Jokes from the Pubs of Ireland

James N. Healy

D1392890

MERCIER PRESS

MERCIER PRESS

Trade enquiries to CMD DISTRIBUTION,
55a Spruce Avenue, Stillorgan Industrial Park, Blackrock, Dublin

20 19 18 17 16 15 14

To Denis, Tony, Mick and all the boys with whom I have had
such laughs over the lengthening years.

No character in this book bears any resemblance whatever to a
human being.

Printed in Ireland by Colour Books Ltd.

I was having a quiet pint when two fellows staggered through
the door of the bar, and they carrying a third fellow between
them. Up they comes to the counter. 'Two pints and two
chasers,' sez one of 'em to Harry, 'and hurry, because we're on
the road to Limerick, and we're running out of petrol.' 'Bub-
illy-bubb-ubilly-bub,' sez the third fella, and with that he
collapses on the floor, out to the world.

Harry peers over the counter, and has a squint at him lying
on the floor. 'Hurry up, Mike,' sez the second fella, who was
also a bit full, to Harry, who's a bit proud of his Christian
name and wouldn't appreciate being called Mike. ''Tis a long
ould road.' 'What about your pal?' sez Harry without a touch
of the sarcasms, and nodding at your man on the ground.

'Nothin' for him,' sez the first fella aggressively, '—he's
drivin'.'

*   *   *

I love ferreting and I often used go out with the lads of a
Sunday, but I was never lucky enough to have a talking ferret.

Harry swears that a fella who used to come in had one, but
in the end he had to scare him away, because he frightened the
other customers.

This fella was always boasting about the ferret, and we were
always saying, 'Well, we'll be going out with our wan on
Sunday — why don't you bring the great talking ferret with
you, and he can tell us where the rabbits are — Ha, ha, ha, and
so on and so forth.' 'Well,' sez this fella, ''tis how we can't go
out on Sunday, 'cos the ferret has influenza: but,' — rather
vaguely — 'some Sunday when he's better and 'tis fine, we'd
love to.' We didn't see him for a long time after that, and it
became a recognised joke in Harry's bar about the liar who
said he had a talking ferret, but in he comes one night as bold
as brass, with a bit of the staggers on him. 'Half-a-whisky for
me,' sez he, 'and a half-pint of Bass for the ferret.'

'I'm sorry,' sez Harry, with a wink to those of us who were
around, 'but we don't serve dumb animals.' 'Who's dumb?' sez
your man, 'if you won't serve me friend, hump you Harry.'
'And that,' sez the ferret popping his head out of your man's
breast pocket, 'goes for me too.'

The Tax office is it? Tell them to open all the windows, and we'll be along in the morning.

Ham 77

TEMPTATION

'I've a terrible temptation to have another pint,' sez Dinny to Miko.

'Well there's only wan way to get rid of temptation,' sez Miko.

'What's that?' sez Dinny.

'Give in to it of course,' sez Miko. 'Two more pints please.'

'Anyway,' he continued, attacking the new pint as if his life depended on it, 'temptation is a terrible persistent thing and unless you get rid of it you won't be able to avoid it.'

Miko has a philosophy about temptation although he mightn't use such a high-falutin' word. 'You might as well make the most of temptation,' he says, 'while you can't avoid it, 'cos when you get older 'twill avoid you.'

'But don't ya have no conscience?' sez Dinny.

'Well, 'tis like dis,' sez Miko, laying one large hand around a cold pint, 'the Lord occasionally speaks to me about me goings on; but sometimes I talks right back to Him, and half the time he lets me have me own way, so fill 'em up again, Harry! — and wan for the pianist.'

'Why does he play the piano?' sez Dinny. 'He used to have a guitar.'

'There was one disadvantage.'

'What was that?'

'You can't stand a pint on a guitar.'

'Lor', I didn't think he drank hardly at all.'

'Drink? Are ye coddin'? He soaks it up like a alligator. 'Twasn't 'till he went home sober one night and the wife knew he wasn't normal that she realised he drank at all so, you see, he got into trouble the wan night he didn't give in to temptation.'

So that's the way that Miko deals with temptation.

*   *   *

Christmas comes but once a year and when it comes we have a raffle in our pub. Last year a young chap — we'll call him Chris — who comes in an odd time, had just been married and was so broke before Christmas that he couldn't even buy a ticket. However, after Christmas I met him and he was in great form. He told me he had had a smashing Christmas. He got hold of the butcher's dog and blew him up with the bellows; then he brought the dog to the butcher and said; 'This dog came into our house and eat the poor little turkey we could afford for Christmas, a cake, and knocked over our bottle of wine on the way out, and what are you going to do about it?'

The butcher said: 'Well, if I gave you a few of these cigars, one of the cakes my wife made, a nice round of corned beef, this

5

box of chocolates left by a friend, and couple of quid, would that do?'

'That will do fine,' said Chris. 'Thank you very much.'

Fair enough—as he said to me—'We had a smashing Christmas.'

A few days later I was passing the butcher's shop and, seeing the window broken I went in to sympathise.

'Hallo,' said I. 'Did somebody break in?' — thinking of the villians who are going around nowadays.

'Ah, no,' said the poor man, 'the fire was going out this morning and when I went to get the bellows to blow it up the poor dog, who's usually as quiet as a lamb, jumped out the bloody window.'

*   *   *

Every Christmas for years Mrs O'Brien, who comes from Knocknagorrery in the hills beyond Macroom used to come in to the city hospital regular as clockwork to give birth to her annual child. Her husband, who is a fairly rough character called Corny would spend the three days in Harry's anxiously waiting, quietly sipping away, and then when the news came through he would go berserk on the hard stuff. This year, as we were helping him out the door, Harry said: 'I suppose we'll be seeing you again as usual next year, Corny?'

'No, boss,' says the bold Con. 'Dis is the last time. Me wife and I have just found out what's been causing it.'

*   *   *

The fellow from Chippers circus called in again; he must have liked us or maybe 'twas the free drink. He said he was passing through and he told us about the octopus.

This fellow brought along a talking octopus with him and said it could play the piano, the guitar, and the piccolo. He had human beings playing these things already but he thought it would be a novelty if he could get the octopus to play the bagpipes. 'O.K.,' said the octopus, or at least seemed to nod like, so he borrowed one from the Carrigaline pipe band, and locked the octopus in a room with it all night, thinkin' he could figure it out for himself. Yerra man, there wasn't a sound all night except for an occasional groan from the pipes so first thing in the morning he opened the door and found the octopus inside looking pretty bate out, and the bagpipes beside him not looking much better. He was a bit angry.

'Haven't you learned to play it yet,' sez he to the octopus.

'Play it?' sez the octopus. 'Is that what I was supposed to do? And me trying to seduce the bloody thing all night!'

*　　　*　　　*

We never know whether the man from Chipper's is pulling our leg. They got a new act, he told us; acrobats. In order to make himself more supple the man had his spine removed. The act was successful but his wife had to take him home every night in a bucket.

They filled his spine with mercury but in the hot weather he went up to nine foot two. Then in the cold snap he went down to six inches, and the circus cat got him.

*　　　*　　　*

And fellows come in with short cracks sometimes like:

Did you hear about the fella who was a rear-admiral in the Irish Naval Service and worked his way round to the front? Haw! Haw! Haw!

or

Did you hear about the old lady in the train on the way from Dublin to Cork who was sitting opposite a Scotsman wearing a kilt? He fell asleep, and when he woke up she said: 'That's a nice Pekinese you've go there.' 'That's no' a Pekinese,' said he. 'That's ma' sporran.' 'Oh dearie me, so that's it,' said the old lad. 'I fed it twice with a biscuit but it took no notice.'

*　　　*　　　*

Did you hear about the Film Star who called his baby Oscar because he thought it was his best performance of the year?

*　　　*　　　*

There was a fellow who went to the doctor with a pain in his left leg, and said, 'What will I do?' The doctor said – 'Limp'.

What a wonderful thing is the flea
You can't tell a he from a she
But he can, and she can —
Whoopee!

*   *   *

Dinny was standing in the street the other day when an English chap came up to him and said; 'I say old chap, could you show me the way to the nearest boozer?'
Says Dinny, hopefully; 'You're looking at him.'

*   *   *

Chris came into Harry's the other night, and we were all agog to see him because we heard that his mother-in-law had been missing three days.
    'Any news of her?' said Dinny.
    'No,' says Chris, non-committal.
    'Did you give her description to the police?'
    'How could I do that?'
    'Why not?'
    'Nobody would believe it.'
and with that he went on drinking his pint.

*   *   *

Little Johnny with a shout
Gouged the baby's eyeballs out
Jumped on them to make them hop
Mother said: 'Now Johnny, stop.'

*   *   *

THE LADIES

'Lady Drivers!' said Billo morosely the other evening.
'I was driving back from Fermoy today and one of 'em shouted to me, "Pig!" as I passed her going at ninety—'
'What did you do?' said Miko.
'I shouted back, "Hag!" and ran over a pig.'

*   *   *

STOP PRESS

We have just heard that a lady prominent in Cork's night clubs has disappeared and hasn't been obscene since.

A nice girl is one who whispers
sweet nothing-doings in your ear, says Joe.

*   *   *

A psychologist is a man who watches
everybody else when a beautiful girl
comes into the room.

*   *   *

NOTICE HUNG IN HARRY'S THE OTHER NIGHT—
'Honest workman with corkscrew would like to hear of a
widow with a pub!'

*   *   *

Chris' weakness is for the horses. He can't resist a gamble, and
it worries the wife like hell. He was at home the other night
with his nose stuck in the sporting press, having an occasional
look up at their infant who looks like a tomato, but of whom
he is very proud, and who at that time was slobbering around
in a play pen. Turning to the missus he said: 'Baby's nose is
running again.' His wife snapped at him: 'Don't you ever think
of anything but horse races?'
Sometimes you can't be right.

*   *   *

We have a wild character who comes into Harry's. He is a
young fella named Billo with more money than he has earned,
and a red face, which isn't from sunshine.
The other day he was caught gunning his Mercedes (mark
the word) the wrong way down the South Mall by a guard,
who asked him where he was going.
'I'm not too sure,' sez Billo through a kind of a mist, 'but
wherever it is I must be late, 'cos everybody seems to be
coming back already.'

*   *   *

'I met this wan at a dance last week,' said Billo, 'a real posh
one. I asked her could I drive her home, and when we got to
her flat she asked me in for a cup of coffee. Well coffee wasn't
much in me line, but I thought there might be a hope that

9

she'd have an oul' bottle somewhere so in I goes. Yirra man we weren't sitting down when she ups and says, "I'm going to get into a negliggy and relax". I didn't know what she was talking about but in half a minute she comes in in a nighty and sits next to me on the settee. Then she put the lights out.'

'What happened then?'

'Well I can take a hint. I knows when I'm not wanted. I got me hat and went home.'

* * *

CHRIS' KID IS A CHIP OFF
THE OLD BLOCK

WHO TOLD THE MILKMAN
THAT WE HAD SWITCHED
TO BEER?

Haven't seen old Billy the Buff around recently. His idea of a real good time was to consume as much as possible in as short a time as he could and get blind drunk as a result. After mumbling incoherently for a while he would usually pass out quietly and would then be no more trouble to anyone until he had to be swept out at closing time. Barty was his pal, and would always stand up for him when people commented facetiously on old Billy's habits. 'I see the Buff's dead drunk again,' said one pious old parishioner one night as he observed Billy's form recumbent on a bench. 'He's not drunk,' said Barty truculently enough. 'I just seen him move.'

*   *   *

One day the same old pious reformer, Burko the bank manager, being fond of a half-one himself, decided to do some reforming on old Bill. The Buff was sitting glumly eeking out a pint because he hadn't the money to buy another one. 'I am sure,' said Burko unctiously, 'that if you made a big effort and gave up drinking and smoking that you would live longer.'

Billy blinked his bleary eyes and paused before replying in a wheezy voice: 'I dunno about that — But it would seem longer.'

*   *   *

Not many inhabitants of Harry's Bar are too religious, but when a mission comes on a good number rally around and attend.

The bar fills up around nine o'clock, and is often much fuller than usual since the wives drove their men out to be holy because they have a chance, which they sometimes might otherwise not have, of lowering a couple on the way home.

The irreligious are in before that, and in the comfortable seats; they sometimes, at least on the surface, like to be represented as being a little derisive of the dutiful ones.

'Well,' said Joe, with a wink all round, to Mr Burke, the bank manager who never does have much to say, and is one of those whom we don't see often, 'what did the fellow tonight have to say about sin?'

Burko looked into his glass rather glumly. 'He's against it,' said he, before polishing off the half-one, and heading home to the wife.

Burko is of course very neat and that night he had a small brown paper parcel with him. He put it on the counter. It was the family Bible, but Ned wasn't to know that.

'Anything breakable in it?' sez he, with the usual wink.

'Only the Ten Commandments.' sez Burko.

*　　　*　　　*

Young Robert, who is a nice fellow, was looking rather down in the dumps that night, as he was sitting in front of a glass of lager so I asked him what was wrong. He replied that he had had a quarrel with his girl friend.

'In that case,' said Joe who was among those present, and who is a married man of some years, 'you'd better go along and apologise.'

'Why should I do that?' sez Robert. 'We might have had an argument, but I was right – she was in the wrong.'

'In that case,' said Joe, 'you'd better bring her a box of chocolates as well.'

*　　　*　　　*

Naturally when conversation starts in the bar it sometimes turns to personalities, and it is not infrequent that reputations are torn to shreds.

'Oh I don't know,' said Robert, the other night when we had been tearing old Burko the bank manager to shreds behind his back, 'he's not bad – there's one thing; he's always very polite to his inferiors.' Robert is a charitable young man.

'Yes,' said Joe, who isn't, 'but where does he find them?'

*　　　*　　　*

12

Burko paid one of his visits to us the other night (it was the wife's night out to Bridge) and held forth on all topics over the single scotch for an hour before departing without giving any of us much chance to join in.

He also devastated us with what he usually regards as dry wit. It's very dry, for 'tis seldom he stands a-round.

'Miserable bugger,' grumbled Ned when at last Burko took his leave.

'He fancies himself as a wit,' said Robert, always prepared to be charitable.

'He's only half right,' said Ned.

* * *

Burko was holding forth on the subject of young people being immoral—a favourite and very boring subject of his.

'I consider the conduct of the younger generation,' said he in his pompous way, 'highly improper. I am given it on the best authority that many of the young people of today sleep together even before they are married. I can assure you that there was nothing improper in my case. I certainly never slept with my wife before I was married to her—Did you?' This last was aimed suddenly and accusingly in the direction of Joe who was listening with an ear and a half and looking over the glass at Harry with one of his eyes.

'I dunno,' said Joe with great rapidity, 'what was her maiden name?'

* * *

Burko was indignant about that and moved down to the other end of the counter. He didn't speak to Joe for three days until Harry asked them to move together one day when only the two of them were in the bar.

'I hope you don't mind,' said Joe.

'Don't apologise, my dear fella,' said Burko with the utmost politeness, 'after all I have never been bored by half as much as you bore me.'

* * *

MR BUCKLEY, I'D LIKE YOU TO MEET MR BURKE — AND IT WILL SAVE ME THE HELL OF A LOT OF TROUBLE IF YOU DO

Billy the Buff had been warned to be home by the missus but someone had stood him an extra couple so he had lingered, and was a bit mussy. Just the same the missus was on his conscience.

'Have you the time?' said he to Harry.

'Sure—'

'Thanks.'

Eventually Harry told Billy that it was half past seven and he really ought to be going home.

'Wha' time?' sez Billy.

'Half-seven.'

'That's funny,' sez Billy huzzled.

'What's funny?'

'I've been getting different answers all day.'

Eventually when they got him out of the pub there were two nuns coming towards him. Since Billy was just standing there swaying one walked either side of him. We found him there still scratching his head.

'Now, how in the hell did she do that?' was his remark.

*　　　*　　　*

Joe told us he had been ticked off by his boss in the garage where he works for continually coming in late.

'Look here Buckley,' said the boss that morning, 'don't you know what time we start work around here?'

'No, sir,' says Joe very politely. 'They're always at it by the time I arrive.'

ABROAD (or 20 miles from Cork)

There's all sort of talk about Africa lately in Harry's, and most of the fellas have solutions about Rhodesia, and Algeria and Mr Amin and the rest. So lately when a fellow came in who had spent a few years, or it might have been days, in Africa we all crowded round to hear what he had to say. He was there when Mr Kissinger went along to Idi Amin with a solution of all the problems, and found himself at a great reception at

HUZZANGA

which all the local chiefs, and a lot of pretty tough looking blacks with spears, were present and after a hearty meal of he didn't know what, Mr K. stood up, more than a little nervous, to try and make friends and to tell the savages all about the outside world, and how we want to make peace with everybody, etc., etc., and to screw them for as much as we can.

'Out there,' said old K., 'we love our fellow men.' At this all the savages raised their spears and gave a loud ringing cry of 'Huzzanga!'

Encouraged by this reception he continued, 'We treat others as we would have them treat us.'

'Huzzanga,' cried the natives.

'We are peaceful,' he shouted, further encouraged.

'Huzzanga,' said the natives, louder than ever.

With a tear running down his cheek, Old Kiss. ended his fine speech, 'We come to you as friends; as brothers. Trust us, open to us your arms, your houses, your hearts—what do you say?'

The air shook with one long mighty, 'Huzzanga!'

Much contented Dr K. then began chatting with Amin, who had woken up and was groping for the bottle.

'I see you have cattle here,' he said in a winning manner, and wishing to show interest in local agricultural matters. 'They are a species with which I am not familiar—may I come and inspect them?'

'Certainly—you come this way,' said Idi A. 'But be careful not to step in the Huzzanga.'

*   *   *

This fellow also told us about how you can now go to Africa on what is called a Safari (not Sari which is a kind of woman's nightshirt they wear during the day in India or some place) and said there were two fellows from Meath or some other place in Ireland too far away from Cork to be civilised named Gunning and Melia who went on one of these Saris or Safaris.

When they had made camp at night Gunning says to Melia that he would go for a walk.

Melia said that that was dangerous with lions and whatnot around, but Gunning said that they were all tame now, it said it in the brochure, and, moreover he bet Melia a pound that he would be back within the hour, safe and sound. However an hour passed and then another one, and there was no sign of your man, none at all. Melia was right worried, but eventually there was a noise outside of someone falling over a bucket, and Melia sat up in bed. 'Is that you Gunning?' said he With that a large shaggy lion stuck his nose through the flap of the tent and growled: 'You know that fella Gunning? – well he owes you a pound.'

*   *   *

'That reminds me,' said Joe, 'that I met a fellow the other day who actually had never heard the original Shaggy Dog story.'

'What's the original Shaggy Dog story?' says Billo.

'What's a shaggy dog story?' said Burko.

'Well I'll tell you,' sez Joe. 'You see in medieval times there were castles all over the country.'

'Like Blarney?' says Miko.

'Like Blarney,' sez Joe, 'only bigger. Well these castles had knights and fine ladies in them and flags flying, and they had a thing called chivalry which meant the men didn't bash the women about. They also had a law of hospitality whereby if a knight came knocking at a castle door at night he would be given a bed and a meal. Well one very stormy night there was a loud knocking at this castle door and when the watchman looked over the battlements, he saw a battered looking knight, but instead of riding a horse he was on a large Shaggy Dog.

'Let me in,' sez he.

Now the watchman would normally let in a knight on a horse, but he had never seen a knight on a Shaggy Dog before. 'We're full up,' sez he. 'Ah, come on,' sez the knight. 'No,' says your man, with more confidence. 'We're full up; no room, try the castle down the road.'

'Ah,' sez the knight, 'you wouldn't leave a knight out on a dog like this.'

*   *   *

THE SHAGGY DOG
* * *

Chris wouldn't be outdone by the fellow with the stories about Africa:

'I knew a fellow,' he said, 'who went for his holidays to the North Pole.'

'Don't be stupid,' said Burko. 'They can't get up to that place, not to mind having holidays there.'

''Twas on the latest Joe Murphy list I got,' said Joe.

'Go on,' said Burko to Chris; anything would be better than having to listen to Joe.

'Well it was so cold up there,' said Chris, 'that when they threw a glass of water up into the air it froze and stayed there like a satellite.'

Silence.

'What's more,' he continued, 'the glass froze too, and the whole lot stayed up there in a great big lump.'

'Jazus,' said Miko.

'That's absurd,' said Burko. 'The ice would fall on your head, what about the law of gravity?'

Chris was stumped but only for a moment —

'It was so cold,' he said impressively, 'that the law of gravity was frozen too.'

*   *   *

'One day,' said Miko, 'a cannibal caught a Baptist Preacher looking at Teleffs Éireann in Central Africa—'

'How could you get Teleffs Éireann in Central Africa?' scoffed Joe.

'A bloody sight easier than you could get the B.B.C. in Cork,' said Miko. 'Will you listen? The cannibal was hungry; the Baptist, who was listening to 'On the Land', was so enthralled that he never knew what hit him until he woke up in a pot of boiling water. When he was cooked the cannibal ate him. Later that night he got tummy-ache, and complained to his wife. She dosed him with Syrup of Figs. He went out, and was some while away. 'What kep' you, Luther?' says the wife, whose name was Bridget. 'I got sick,' says he, 'and I threw up the Baptist.'

'Ah well,' says she, 'you can't keep a good man down.'

'Yes,' said Luther pensively, 'I couldn't have luck, Biddy. I should have stuck to Jesuits.'

*   *   *

'Talking about that,' said Joe, 'did you hear they're going to convert Ian Paisley?'

'Is that so?' said Chris.

'Yes, they're going to bring him down to the next international at Lansdowne Road and kick him over the crossbar.'

CORK & DUBLIN

A Dublin man died and went straight to his eternal home. Looking around he commented:
'I never expected Heaven to be so like O'Connell Street.'
'Joxer,' the gatekeeper informed your man, 'this isn't Heaven.'

*　　　*　　　*

'I love going to the Dublin Zoo,' said Basil. 'Whenever I'm in the big city I take the opportunity to go, nice peaceful atmosphere, good place for lunch, and I love to watch the animals get up to their tricks.'
'Well it can be a bit embarrassing sometimes,' said Michael P. joining in, 'especially as some of their tricks can be a bit hard to explain with young ladies around, if you know what I mean. For want of something to do I took Jill before we were married. You know Jill, she's a bit innocent.'
'Dumb as hell.'
'Yes. Above all she wanted to see the monkeys, but when we got to their cages the keeper said they were nearly all inside because it was the mating season. "Do you think they'd come out if I threw them a few peanuts," sez Jill with her big open eyes. The keeper who was a bit of a down-to-earth Dubliner took one look at her and he sez, sez he, "Would *you*, Miss?"'

*　　　*　　　*

Somebody told a Dublin Jackeen that they were sending up elephants in the next satellite going to the moon. 'I suppose,' sez Joxer, 'they'll be there to make Trunk calls.'

*　　　*　　　*

A Jackeen came into Harry's the other Sunday while waiting to catch the train back to Dublin after a football match. He had an unlit cigarette dangling from his mouth.
'Got a light, Mac?' sez he to Burko, who doesn't appreciate being addressed with such familiarity.
'No,' says Burko with perfect politeness, 'but I've got a heavy overcoat.'

The Dublin fellas say that when a Corkman goes to Dublin the first thing he does is throw a stone in the Liffey and if it floats he goes home again.

*   *   *

'C'mere,' says Miko aggressively, 'wid de pollusion in de Liffey it might float at dat!'

*   *   *

The Cork fellas say that the best thing in Dublin nowadays is the road to Cork.

      ('an' I wish to Jaysus that some of ye would find it,'
               sez the Dublin Jackeen)

AT THE HOBBLEDY-HOY

The Hobbledy-Hoy is a rather posh pub that I go into occasionally. Well—posh in the sense that the fellows all wear ties and think themselves a bit better than their betters.

They are also fond of their sense of humour, and think it rather superior.

I met Trevor there when last in. He was just back from Paris, and was regretting that he hadn't gone twenty years before.

'When Paris was really Paris, eh?' I felt obliged to say.

'No,' says a voice from down the line, 'when Trevor was really Trevor.'

Fair enough.

*   *   *

'Did you see the bathing beauties there,' said Gurruld, who's a bit of a wit.

'They've no bathing beauties there,' says Trevor (looking a bit puzzled just the same, as if it was something he had missed and shouldn't have), 'you'd have to go to the Côtée Jure for that or the Costy dell Sull.'

'Do you like them, though?' persisted Gurruld with a wink at his friends.

'I dunno,' retorts Trevor, back on familiar ground, and quick as a flash, 'I never bathed one.' Trevor laughed anyway.

The same Trevor is a bit inclined for the birds.

He met a new one lately, but they didn't have much of a conversation.

'Since this is our first date I must tell you that I don't go in for necking, — is that clear?' was her opening remark.

'Yes.'

'Good! Now where shall we go?'

'Home.'

He meant it too.

*　　*　　*

However he didn't get rid of the same girl too easily, for she probably thought that with his fine clothes (mostly on tick) and his air of being the son of a merchant prince that he was worth a bit more than he is, so she kept ringing him up, and once she introduced him to her father. 'I think she must have a bit of a crush,' said Gurruld when he heard it.

'Take care she doesn't take it to heart.'

'I'd be more nervous like,' said Trevor after a pause, and in his best Cork drawl, 'that she might take it to court.' ('And that's more than you could do with her, you ruffian,' said Gurruld to the others under his breath.)

'What did the father say to you?' asked G. aloud.

'He asked me whether my intentions were honourable or dishonourable.'

'And what did you say?'

'That I didn't know I had a choice!'

I think that's what finished it.

*　　*　　*

Basil is one who believes in the direct approach.

Recently, at a cocktail party, he met a sophisticated girl from Dublin who was new to the Cork scene.

He's not slow in getting off the mark either; besides she wasn't bad looking and he knew that Trevor, Denis and some of the others were hovering around.

'I'm a man of few words,' said he, with the air of an executive. 'Will you, or won't you?'

. The sophisticated young lady did no more than raise an eyebrow. 'Your house, or my flat?' she snapped back.

'Well,' said Basil, who's not used to getting the direct approach in return and was unsettled by it. 'If there's going to be an argument, let's forget the whole thing.'

* * *

CHRIS' KID IS NOW OLD ENOUGH TO EMBARRASS NEW NEIGHBOURS

GOT ANY KIDS MY AGE?

Basil was talking about his weekend experiences, but what he really wanted to do was to casually drop into the conversation the fact that his new platinum blonde friend from Dublin, Samantha, whom he had met at the cocktail party, had been with him.

'I found this most interesting piece of ore on the Kerry Mountains,' said Basil, producing a scruffy-looking lump of rock from his pocket, 'Samantha said she didn't know what it was, but she wondered if it might be valuable.'

'Take it to a metallurgist,' suggested Gurruld.

'What's a metallurgist?'

'He's a man who can look at a platinum blonde and tell whether she is Virgin metal or a common ore.'

* * *

'She's an experienced woman,' said Basil, whose youth sometimes gives him away, 'not like the others. I don't know what approach to make.'

'The best way to approach a woman with a past is with a present,' said Michael P.

* * *

'You want to handle her carefully,' said Trevor, 'the only time I met her was at a "do" at the Yacht Club. I asked her for a dance.'

'What did she say?' said Basil anxious to mark his card.

'She told me she wouldn't dance with a child.'

'That was rough! What did you say in reply?'

'That I was sorry, but I didn't realise her condition.'

* * *

THE HOBBLEDY-HOY BOYS SONG

(Air: *My Bonny lies over the ocean*)

Martinis, my girls, are deceiving
Take two at the very most.
Take three and you're under the table
Take four and you're under the host.

Basil was sitting on the verandah of the Yacht Club, asking the best way to teach a girl to swim:

Trevor: 'Well, first you put one arm around her waist.'

Basil: 'It's my sister!'

Trevor: 'Oh! Just push her off the pier.'

*   *   *

It was closing time at the Hobbledy-Hoy. Gurruld felt the party time might be continued so he asked a few of us to come to his house for drinks. 'You know the address,' he said to Trevor. 'Just push the bell with your elbow.'

'With my elbow?' said Trevor. 'What's wrong with my finger?'

'Well, now, Trev. old boy,' said Gurruld as he hitched up his trousers and departed, 'you'll not be coming to the party empty-handed, now will you? Come on lads.' Touché.

THE GOLF CLUB

I don't get into the Golf Club bar very often, but it's a great place to stand with a bottle (no pints allowed) and have a look through the window at the other fellows making egits of themselves.

We can hear the conversation from the fourteenth tee through the clubhouse window. It's about 180 yards to the green; a short hole. The other day a particular eegit who's come up in the world recently was standing on the tee. I didn't know what sort of a golfer he was, but I'll say this for him — he was very well dressed.

'This should be good for a drive and a putt,' sez he, in his best Cork gurr, to the caddy, and maybe he knew we were listening. 'Awrite,' sez Jerry Mac, who was carrying the bag. With that your man hit the ball a flake and it went about two yards, trickling along the ground.

There was silence for a minute and, shure God help us, I hope your man didn't hear the guffaw from the club house.

The caddy was chewing gum and he didn't move a muscle of his face except to get out the putter and say to your man: 'I'm afraid it's going to be the hell of a putt, sir.'

Meanwhile a wife was having a go off her husband in the bar. 'You think so much of your blasted golf game,' she was proclaiming, 'that you don't even remember when we were married.'

'Of course I do darling,' he said, with the greatest sincerity. 'It was the day I sank that 40 yard putt!'

* * *

The wives play too, not half they don't. They had a medal competition or some such a week or so ago. It was a very wet day, and Terence kept his wife company. While she was getting soaked out on the course he was sitting in the bar drinking whiskies. She was very wet when she got in, and what's more she was in vile humour because she had shot an 82 nett, well down the list, while Gladys with whom she was playing, and whom she detests, had a 71 and a very good chance of winning the watch. 'What'll you have,' said Gladys as they got into the bar, and she said it with the air of a conquering hero. The hubby had time to look around from the story he was telling, which was a lot of bloody lies about how he won the stroke play competition some years ago with a putt right across the 18th green. 'Are you wet, dear?' said he, most solicitously. She didn't hear him, or at least didn't pretend to. 'I'd better go to the bar and console the missus,' said he, and arrived there just to get in at the end of Gladys' round. 'Are you wet, dear?' he goggled at his wife, and jogged her elbow just as she was about to down her gin-and-tonic. She reached down to the bag of clubs which, against all rules, she had brought into the bar and selected a no. 8. She then hit him a belt around the ear-hole with the club. 'Are you hurt, dear?' sez she.

* * *

'How did the trouble start?' said the club secretary to Trevor after it had been reported that a lady member had slapped his face at the Golf Club 'Do' — Trevor doesn't play golf, but likes the parties. 'Well she asked me to play a round,' said Trevor. 'I didn't know she meant Golf.'

* * *

Michael P. and the wife aren't getting on too well, and perhaps that is why he seems happier on the golf course than at home. 'Golf, golf, golf,' she wailed, as he started to throw the clubs into the old Merc. last Sunday. 'I really believe I'd drop dead if you spent one Sunday at home.'

'Now dear,' he answered, 'there's no use talking to me like that. You know you can't bribe me.'

Fore!

*　　*　　*

Michael P. was having a friendly round the other Wednesday with a business acquaintance whom he didn't know very well, but with whom he was hoping to do a deal. A couple of ladies ahead of them were foothering around the course, losing balls and having a chat, and generally holding up the two boyos.

'I wonder would you mind,' said Michael P., 'going ahead to those two ladies and asking them to let us through. I don't want to shout 'fore', it would be embarrassing for me. You see one of them is my wife, and the other is my mistress.'

'I don't mind at all,' said me man who had fairly recently come from Dublin to sample the delights of living in a really culchured city, and he proceeded to amble up the course. As soon as he got within twenty yards of the ladies, who were by that time discussing jumpers and having a chat about golf fashions in general, he suddenly stopped and then came back without speaking to them, but with a rather red face.

'What's up?' said Michael P.

'I'm sorry,' said your man, who's a bit short sighted, 'I'm afraid I'd have the same problem.'

*　　*　　*

He did not drink, or smoke or swear
His morals were not bad.
Nor did he live a century —
He only felt he had.

HUNTIN' AND SHOOTIN'

I have never gone hunting, because in the first place I could never afford a horse, and in the second place I sometimes find it difficult to distinguish between the horses who hunt and the ladies who ride them; and I would hate to be talking to a horse when I thought it was a lady, or versa visa, as they often even sound the same.

However, it is a fine sight to watch the hunt setting out in their red—that is to say pink—coats, and some of them—presumably a sort of second division—in black, and a very good venue to watch this occasion,from a pub on St Stephen's morning, where also you can wait with much pleasure and a couple of pints for them to straggle back an hour or so later. It doesn't take long for many of the fellas in the hunt have a head on Stephen's morning as well as lesser mortals, and after a field or two jogging up and down on a horses's back it begins to seem more pleasant to be back in the pub with a gin and tonic rather than falling into another couple of muddy ditches on the heights.

A few years ago there was this fellow around who took whatever opportunity he could to impress on other people what he thought his proper station in society should be.

On this particular week he had a few friends over from England to stay with him, and he thought that one of the best ways to impress them would be to hire a couple of nags from the farmer down the road, and take them hunting. They were a bit late arriving for the meet, and the hunt had already gone up the hill and off to the right by the time they got there, so having struggled up the hill and about a half-mile past the turn he hailed a couple of County Council workers who were digging up the road, and working very hard leaning on their shovels. 'Whoa!' he said—which for some reason is a word horses are supposed to understand—and then:

'I say, my man, have you seen the gentry go by?' The biggest of them sucked his teeth and rubbed his nose before he gave the slow reply: 'Yes, sur—about twenty years ago.'

* * *

There was a story told too about the day that the huntsman let a bitch in heat go out with the pack of hounds. They found a fox, but the pack travelled off so fast that none of the hunt could keep up with them; so, they trailed along behind, and the huntsman kept asking passers-by, or the odd fellow in a field, whether they had sight or sound of the hounds.

'Did you see e'er a sight of the hounds, Willie?' said he to a farmer he knew.

'Faith then, I did,' said the farmer. 'They were going strong over the breast of the hill yonder, and the fox was lying fifth.'

* * *

Show jumping is another thing people go in for. To tell the truth it must be the most boring thing I have ever witnessed, although the last gymkhana I was at was enlivened by Basil and his friends coming along half-jarred and giving a running commentary. 'Next to go,' he drawled in the manner beloved of B.B.C. and even R.T.E. commentators, 'is Felicity Frump-Foddington who is over from Aux-ford for the day. She's put everything she's got on this horse, and that's quite a weight. Now she's turned, and she's approaching the first jump. Here she comes—and she's over!—by George she's over!

'The horse is still on this side, but *she's* over. She's taken a bit of a tumble but she's alright. Great stuff in Felicity Frump-Foddington—she's one of the Foddingtons of Fiddington-Faddington, you know. But she's alright, you may say she's alright. She's up now, and she's walking away; oh, no—that's the horse.

'But Felicity's up too, she has a slight limp, but she's walking away. She had a crash helmet on, but unfortunately she had it on the wrong end. . .'

After that a stuffy old fellow with bucked teeth came and said, 'Ahy think yah des-tay-bing the hor-ses,' so we left, and spent the rest of the afternoon in the more congenial atmosphere of the pub, being ministered to by the round and smiling face of our genial host.

* * *

HUNTING LADY

FELICITY FRUMP- FODDINGTON
- ALSO USED FOR SHOW-JUMPING

'Didn't she never see a litter of white rats before?'

* * *

'I do me best to please me ma-in-law,' said Chris, 'but I can seldom succeed. I even remembered her last birthday, and brought her along a bunch of flowers. As soon as she opened the door and looked at me the flowers withered. I wouldn't mind, but they were plastic.'

* * *

BACK TO HARRY'S

When I got in the other night there were three unbelievably decrepit old grey haired men sitting at the bar. God help us I bought them a drink, because firstly, I thought they'd got out of some home for old folks, and secondly there was no one else around to talk to. They were friendly old boys. 'I'm 86,' says the first one accepting a lemonade, 'and I wouldn't be here today if I hadn't scorned alcohol, late hours and the sinful enticement of the opposite sex.' The second old boy went so far as to have a coca-cola. 'I'm 93,' he piped up, 'and I owe me years to a strict diet of molasses, bananas, brown bread and mother's milk.'

'When I was 18,' mumbled the third fella, the most decrepit of the three, 'my father said I should enjoy life as much as I could; smoke black cigars, drink nothing but the hard stuff, and go out with a different woman every night, and,' he added, 'that's exactly what I've done.'

'Incredible,' said the first, taking another sip of the lemonade.

'Amazing,' comes in the second, nibbling at the coke.

'Marvellous,' said I, 'and how old are you?'

'Twenty-six,' said your man, collapsing on the floor as he reached for the large one I'd bought him.

* * *

The Sales in Patrick Street are a great attraction every year, but most of the fellows don't come in to Harry's around that time because either they have to go round with the missus to carry the parcels, or else she has bought so many things that they are broke.

However, Chris took advantage of the sales after Christmas this year to buy himself a new pair of pyjamas. They were striking all right—bright red collar, blue cuffs and the rest of them looking like rather violent puce wallpaper. When Harry turned the lights down a bit we were able to look at them all right, so we all pinched and pulled at them and admired them in turn.

Corny O'Brien was up from Knocknagorrery as well, for the

usual reason, habit having got the better of his new found knowledge. 'What's them?' he asked when Chris proudly held them up in front of his nose.

'Pyjamas.'

'Pyjamas,' echoed Corny. 'What's they for?'

'Why you wear them at night,' sez Burko, 'why don't you take advantage of the sales to buy yourself a pair?'

'God, no sir,' sez Dinny, 'sure I don't go nowhere except to bed at nights.'

*   *   *

Chris however told us that while he was in a big shop there was a terrible scramble going on because of some special items that were on offer if you could get in quick. 'Yerra man,' sez he, 'they'd tear the clothes off you.'

'When I was there,' said Joe, 'a woman came up to the Lost and Found department and asked, "has anyone turned in a black skirt with five children from two to six hanging on to it?"'

*   *   *

One little boy of five came up to the counter anxiously. 'Have any missing mothers been turned in?' said he.

*   *   *

Chris's mother-in-law gave them a present from the sales of a playpen for the whatever-it-is and heir. Chris was delighted. He even thanked the dear lady. 'It's great,' he told us, 'now I can sit in the playpen every night and read, and the child can't get near me.'

*   *   *

Burko was meant to be catching the evening train to Dublin the other evening and called in to have his little glass on the way since our pub isn't all that far from the railway. Well he left, but didn't allow himself much time, and within half-an-hour was back again.

'Hallo,' said Joe, who isn't always sure when to keep his

32

mouth shut. 'Did you miss the train?'

'No,' snapped Burko, not in the best of humours, 'I didn't like the look of it so I chased it out of the station.'

*　　　*　　　*

Along with that poor old Burko is in domestic trouble. When he got home the other night his wife informed him grimly that the housekeeper had quit.

'She said you spoke to her insultingly over the phone.'

'Ye gods,' said Burko, 'I thought I was talking to you', — that didn't help!

*　　　*　　　*

They had trouble with the gardener too for whatever about old Burko saying unfortunate things, the wife is always interfering.

She accused the gardener of drinking because she has seen his wheel-barrow outside a public house.

He made no reply, but that evening he placed his wheel-barrow outside her door and left it there all night.

DINING OUT

Occasionally I can afford a meal at the Lobster, which is a very pleasant restaurant with a nice bit of mate. Some of the ladies who go there with or without their men are a bit social conscious and make a lot of noise waggling around the bits of false jewellery they bought on the continent.

The woman at the table next to mine the other night was looking across the room at a very attractive and much younger lady.

The husband was having an odd dekko too, but he wasn't advertising the fact.

She leant forward and said to hubby in an audible whisper, 'Doesn't that girl look terrible in that low cut dress.'

He had another look, and mumbled, 'not as far as I can see.'

Then there were two ones at the table on the other side of me having a right gossip, when one starts to have a go off the other.

'She told me,' complained this one, 'that you told her the secret I told you not to tell her.'

'Well,' said the second one, bridling up a bit and annoyed like, 'I told her not to tell you I told her.'

'Oh dear,' sighed the first one, 'then, don't tell her I told you she told me.'

With that the one they were talking about came in. 'Oh, hallo,' said the first of me wans. 'I haven't seen you for a-a-ages. I would hardly have know you – you look so much older.'

'I wouldn't have recognised you either,' said the new arrival, 'except for the hat and dress.'

*　　*　　*

The lady with the sharp nose and fat husband asked for a mixed grill and got it. It contained an egg.

Lady: 'Waitress, this egg looks a bit peculiar? What's wrong with it?'

Waitress: 'Don't ask me, ma'am – I only laid the table.'

*　　*　　*

The lads had been a bit late the night before, having been at a dinner of the 39½ Club, so to complete the night after the morning before, Basil, Trevor, Michael P. and Gurruld did the big thing and went to the Lobster.

'You were in fine voice last night, Basil,' said Trevor.

'We're all good singers in our family.'

'They have to be,' said Gurruld, 'there's no lock on the lavatory door.'

'Music runs in this fellow's family,' continued Gurruld, putting his hand on Basil's shoulder, 'or at least it sort of strolls. His father was going to write a song once, but he never got past the first two bars.'

*　　*　　*

Little Johnny with a grin
Drank up all his mother's Gin
Mother said when he was plastered
Go to bed you little b———.

DOWN ON THE FARM WITH NED THE GOM

I spoke to a man on a farm one day
Who said, 'It don't pay 'cos the hens won't lay.'
Then up came one and gave us a shock
He said, 'I can't lay, for begob I'm a cock'.

*　　　*　　　*

Ned the Gom's father has a farm out at Ballybrisheen. He had
a similar kind of worry because the hens were laying their eggs
in fields all round the district and he could never find them.
Eventually he got the bright idea that he would cross the hens
with parrots. We all thought this was a daft idea until the next
time we were at the farm talking to Ned this peculiar looking
bird came up to say, 'Hey, Ned, where will I drop this wan?'

*　　　*　　　*

They gave us a good lunch that day too, fresh eggs with spuds
in their jackets and lovely lean rashers. Down the farmyard
after lunch we saw a pig come limping with a bandage round
its left rear leg, we were all sympathy and asked Ned if the pig
had had an accident.
'Accident? Yerra Naw!' sez Ned, 'but you wouldn't expect the
old da to kill a whole pig just to get a few rashers for ye?'

*　　　*　　　*

For a joke the next time out we got an ostrich egg and present-
ed it to Ned the Gom. He looked at it for a long time from all
sides, then says he, 'You know what, 'twouldn't take many o'
them to make a dozen.'

35

Robert however, who as I said before is very considerate, has Ned's welfare very much at heart, and doesn't like us to be pulling his leg—even tho' we're not sure sometimes whether it's Ned that's pulling ours.

The other Sunday when we went down to the old fashioned, back-o'-the-woods, absolutely smashing little pub that's in the village down the hill from Ned's place, Bob took Ned aside and said:

'You shouldn't be going around talking like a fool.'

'Yirra for phy wouldn't I?' sez Ned. 'Don't they go around talking like me, haw?'

*   *   *

Burko's wife has taken to having singing lessons, so we see him much more frequently now. He even came down the country with us after the Baagles last Sunday because she was practising that afternoon.

It was the first time he met Ned the Gom, and as usual he had advice to offer.

Sez he to Ned: 'Your methods of cultivation are hopelessly out-of-date. I'd be astonished if you got even ten pounds of apples off that tree.'

'So would I,' said Ned, 'for because it's a pear tree.'

Ned was sporting a new pair of banana-coloured shoes which he bought at the sales in the city. They flopped around a bit.

'What size do you take?' said Robert.

'Well,' said Ned having a look down at the yellow perils, 'eight is me size, but nine's are so comfortable that I got twelves,'

It is hard to dispute with Ned's peculiar kind of personal logic.

*   *   *

We were trying to persuade Ned's father to buy a car.

'I've no munney,' sez he.

'But if you had. . .'

'I'd sooner spend the money on a cow.'

'Yes,' said Robert, ever willing to be helpful, 'but isn't it six miles to the village, and don't the missus and yourself have to go in there to shop. Wouldn't the pair of you look silly riding in there on a cow?'

'Not half as bloody silly,' grumbled the old man, 'as I'd look trying to milk a bloody motorin'-car.'

With these people you can't win.

* * *

Down in the pub after the Baagling exercise was over—which for most of us was mercifully soon—some of the local lads sang the odd ballad, and it reminded Burko of his wife's singing. 'Up to now,' he said, 'she always sang by ear, which didn't surprise me since I never did imagine that such sounds could come out of her mouth. Now, however, since she has commenced training, she is forever what she calls "breaking into song". I feel inclined to tell her that she wouldn't have to break in at all if only she had the right key. But then,' he qualifies, for he will seldom say anything against his ould battleaxe of a wife without trying to correct the impression, 'we're all human,' and then, looking at Ned the Gom lowering a pint, 'with very few exceptions.'

He's not a bad old skin is Burko. There are worse around: I think.

* * *

Billo was driving with his usual haste through Ned the Gom's country and he lost his way.

Looking for someone to guide him he saw Ned walking along the road.

'Hey, Malfunction,' said he with normal politeness, 'which is the road to Macroom.'

'How'd ya know me name was Malfunction?' sez Ned with wide open eyes.

'I guessed it,' sez Billo.

'Well thin,' sez Ned turning into a field, 'you should have no trouble at all guessing the road to Macroom.'

37

NED and the MOTOR-CAR

Eventually we persuaded Ned's dacent oul' Da to buy an ould banger of a car. Ned drove it to market, but the results weren't too brilliant, as he told us in verse:

'Twould drive 'oo mad to be drivin' an ould car along the
    road,
With a store of hins, and chickens an' ducks and drakes and
    bulls and cows and calves for 'oor load
An' 'oo start the car and 'oor drivin' along an' the whole
    bloody lot falls out on the road
'Twould drive 'oo mad, Haw?

'Oo twist the yoke an' jump in quick, and 'oo lands on top
    of the drake
Oh Lord, he bites the sate of 'oor pants, and lets out a
    horrible squake

An' when 'oo turns around again, 'oo find 'oo've squashed
    his bake
'Twould drive 'oo mad, Haw?

'Oo twist the yoke that's called the choke, an' the wheel
    comes off in 'oor hand
'Oo put it on wrong an' she starts goin' back, which 'oo
    cannot understand
An' de back of the car goes through a fence, and the geese
    go back on the land
'Twould drive 'oo mad, Haw?

'Oo chases 'em through a field an' the farmer gives 'oo a run
An' he waves aloft at the sate of 'oor pants a double
    breasted gun
When 'oo reach the car the sheep are pinched
                the cows are mooin'
                the bull is roarin'
                the hens have laid eggs
                the pigs have ate 'em
                the calves have the hump where
                'oor da have bate 'em
Oh, Lor', don't think its fun —
'Twould drive 'oo mad, Haw?

'Oo start the car an' 'oor drivin' along, an' begob 'oo drivin'
    nate
Then she stops with a bump for the engine falls out,
        'And begob,' 'oo say, 'She's bate.'
When 'oo look around the sow have had twelve bonhams on
    the sate
'Twould drive 'oo mad, Haw?

The car is broke for the engine's bust, and it will not start
    nohow
So 'oo ties the bull to the front of the car, an' 'oo ties the
    bull to the cow
Then 'oo hit the bull a flake on the hasp
        He runs like mad
        The hins jump out and fly about
        The bonhams start to squeak and shout

The rope goes bust
An' the bull and the cow are off nohow
An' 'oo sit in the road an' watch their dust
'Oor on 'oor way to the market town drivin' 'oor motor car
But 'oo've lost 'oor bastes, an' the car is broke, an' it will
not take 'oo far
So 'oo gives it a kick, an' 'oo laves it there, and next time
'oo'll go in the donkey car
'Twould drive 'oo mad, Haw?

Well, I suppose we've all felt the frustration of a punctured
tyre or an engine that won't start at the most awkward time.
Cars are grand as long as they go!

* * *

The Government are very anxious for efficient farm methods,
especially since our entry into the E.E.C., so they are sending
inspectors out for almost everything. One arrived down at Ned
the Gom's farm the other day and said he was an inspector deal-
ing with A.I. Ned and his father were out in the fields, so his
ma had to deal with the problem. 'Phfat is A.I.,' said she, 'for
a start.'
'Well-er-Artificial Insemination,' sez the little man in the neat
blue suit and briefcase.
'Oh, come on down to the shed and I'll show you the baste of
a cow,' sez the ma.
So they struggled through the yard and the inspector got
Huzzanga up beyond his bootlaces.
The ma opened the shed, 'There's the Baste,' said she. The
inspector opened his bag, took off his coat and rolled his
sleeve up.
'And,' says the ma, as she left and trying to be helpful,
'you can hang your trousers on the nail.'

* * *

40

ANOTHER DAY AT THE HOBBLEDY HOY

'Trevor is in hospital,' said Gurruld.

'Oh, I'm sorry to hear that,' said Basil. 'Bad and all as he is. How's he getting along?'

'He's taken a turn for the nurse,' said Gurruld.

Nevertheless, having taken a few more, and by that time feeling more charitable to all our fellow neighbours we armed ourselves with a couple of baby bottles of gin and tonic, as well as the regulation half pound of grapes, and we all trooped up to see Trevor, who was sitting up in bed looking glum. He told us he had had a dream the night before, and described it to us.

'I was,' he said, 'driving along the road in a smashing new sports model with this beautiful redhead by my side — a really way-out bird. Here I was keeping an eye out for where I could pull off the road, and park the car. Then in my dream I saw this little side road covered with trees, and the moon shining romantically through the branches; no road lights — that's the place, said I, just the job, so here I am in this dream drawing into this side road with no lights, and my heart is thumping because I am thinking of this red-haired number by my side, who is breathing in my ear and whose perfume is in the air all around me. And then I stop, and I turn to look at her, and there she is looking right back at me, with big shining eyes and tremulous lips, or is it eyes; anyway there she is looking at me and saying: "What are we going to do now?"

'"Yes, yes," getting into the mood and whispering, "what are we going to do now?"

'"How the Hell do I know," says she. "This is your dream!" and with that they woke me for my morning medicine.'

'Not before its time,' said Gurruld, but the rest of us sympathised with Trevor.

'My wife had a nightmare the other night,' said Michael P. who had been silent, but now felt he might continue the theme.

'Was she dreaming of you?' asked Basil, but Michael P. ignored him.

'She dreamt,' he said, 'that she found herself naked at a

cocktail party, and she was very upset, because someone else turned up in the same outfit.'

There was a short silence while the lesser brains were figuring that one out.

'I heard of a very fine strip-tease in Paris,' said Basil, 'in reverse. These two girls come on to a stage with nothing at all on them, and get dressed. It takes an hour and a half.'

'My wife takes that long,' said Michael P.

'Yes, but these two have only three items of clothes — and two of them are shoes.'

*   *   *

'I went to a couple of topless bars when I was in San Francisco last year,' said Gurruld.

'Did you like them?'

'A-a-ah! Once you've seen a couple, you've seen them all.'

*   *   *

'I went on holidays to Germany this year,' said Basil. 'A cruise up the Rhine, and then a week in a family chalet up in the mountains. It was wonderful: the food was superb, the scenery was delightful and the family were most hospitable; but the owner of the place kept introducing me to his daughter. Morning after morning at breakfast he would point to her and say: "That is Verboten!"'

*   *   *

'Did you hear what happened when the Invisible Man met the Invisible Woman?' said Gurruld, apropos of nothing.

'What happened?' said Trevor.

'Nothing — they couldn't find one another.'

*   *   *

And of course there was the short-sighted snake who went out steady with a coil of rope for two years.

HEAVEN IS WHERE YOU FIND IT

There was this old man of eighty-five who married a young girl of twenty. One day he was out for his little toddle of a walk, and as he was coming upstairs to their flat on return he heard scuffling noises and grew very suspicious. Moreoever when he burst into the room his wife was looking very flustered, so he concluded that she had had a man with her. 'Did you have a lover in here with you?' said the old fella, very angry, looking around the room but seeing nobody. 'Oh, no, no!' said the young wife, but at the same time looking guilty as sin. With that the old fellow goes to the window and sees a real Romeo with slick black hair getting into a white sports car just under the window. 'That's your man!' roars the old guy, and with that he picked up the fridge, and threw it out of the window, hitting the fellow in the white car, and killing him on the spot. The old fellow dropped dead too, for you can imagine the effect of picking up a fridge and throwing it out a window at his age. Then both of them proceeded up the golden steps to the Golden Gates, where St Peter was waiting. The romeo-like fellow got there first, even though he had to manage without the car. 'Well? Well-well?' said St Peter, not too politely. 'I was getting into my motor-car,' said the driver, 'with nothing on my mind or conscience, and was just about to pull away from the kerb, when this old man opened a window and threw a fridge at me...' With that the old fellow made it to the top step, and staggered up to the gates. 'Yirra what happened to you?' sez Peter, a bit more sympathetic. 'I saw this posh looking young man getting into a sports car in the street, and I thought he had got out the window having been with my wife, so I threw the fridge at him, and after that everything went black.'

'It all seems to have been a misunderstanding,' said St Peter after a moment's thought. 'Go on in and sort it out for yourselves.'

So, they turned to go into the gates of eternity, and were just entering when a miserable looking little fellow breasted the horizon over the top step, and they all turned to see what had happened to the poor battered little lad. 'What misfortune overcame you at all?' says Peter. 'Well,' sez me little man, leaning against the pillar, and trying to get his breath back, 'I was sitting in this fridge. . .'

*   *   *

The next day St Peter was on duty again, for the poor saint seldom gets time off with people dying all the time. Ian Paisley died and went straight up to Heaven. At least he got as far as the gates until this old lad with the beard came along and stopped him going further. 'Who are yew,' sez the bould Ian, 'and what do yoh mean by standin' in my way?'

'I'm St Peter,' answers the old fella, 'and who do you think you are?'

'I'm Ian Paisley,' shouted your man, 'and as a good Orang'man I claim the right to go straight in—did ye not know I was comin'?'

'I should have guessed it,' sez the saint politely, 'for I heard the explosion but 'twas me morning break and I was having a sandwich and a drop of nectar—but for all that you can't go in for there are one or two things you might have to answer for first.'

'Why should I have to wait,' roars the bold Ian sticking out his lower jaw, 'didn't I have me own kind of a church on earth, and there's no doubt but that I'd get in on a majority decision; this is an insult to the. . .'

'Just the same you'll have to wait,' sez Peter, polite but firm, 'for before we let you in we have to check you out.'

Just then a fine fat old man came puffing up the steps to Heaven. 'I know that man,' sez Ian, 'and you'll surely not let him in before myself, for wasn't he a parish priest on the other side of the border?'

'Oh, begob no,' sez St Peter. 'He'll have to wait too, for there are no borders up here, so will the pair of ye sit over on that piece of a rock there for we're very busy today with large number before ye, and I'll bring ye out the forms to fill up in a moment.' With that he hobbled away back through the gates and closed them after him.

'Forms to fill?' shouts Ian after him, 'you're as bad as the

44

customs posts on the border,' and he got some satisfaction out of saying that, even if it didn't get him any way through the gates.

'Push up on that rock,' he growls to the old P.P., thinking that as they might have to share the same bit of ground for maybe half-an-hour he might as well be polite.

'God bless you, my son,' sez the P.P. who was a bit deaf and bothered, and hadn't much idea of what was going on anyway, 'me feet are killing me after climbing them golden steps.'

Yirra man, they were waiting for well over an hour, and though the P.P. was nodding being, as he said, whacked after the journey, and being used to his little nap in the afternoon; Paisley was getting more and more uneasy, jumping up from the rock to rattle the gates and come back again. Just then there came a muttering in some foreign tongue and a little old rabbi came shuffling up the steps, and right up to the gates where he confidently rang the bell. Sure St Peter opened up the gate the minute he saw who was in it, and with a bare nod let the little old rabbi through.

'What that?' roars our friend Ian, jumping up from the rock and purple with rage, 'you don't mean to say that you'll be lettin' that little old rabbi straight through while leavin' me — and me friend — sittin' here?'

'Will ye keep quiet,' sez St Peter. 'Your turn will come — can't you see that your man is a cousin of the boss's?'

'God bless you, my son,' sez the deaf old priest nodding off again.

*   *   *

DON'T LOOK NOW—
BUT I THINK THEY'RE CLOSING

REMARKS AT CLOSING TIME

Harry: 'I get all odd types here. A fat woman ran in here in tears the other night crying "I've been let down! I've been let down!"'

Us: 'What did you do?'

Harry: 'I said it's all right, love, you can be pumped up again.'

Joe to Chris: 'But do you have home comforts?'

Chris: 'Well—yes; except for meals that is—mind you I'm not saying the wife is a bad cook, but I still believe in prayers before meals.'

* * *

Miko: 'De doctor sent for me de udder day and said, "I don't like de look o' your wife," I said, "to tell de truth neider do I, Doctor, but she's de only wan I got".'

* * *

Burko: 'You expect to get a perfect wife? Could anybody tell me what the qualities of a perfect wife should be?'

Joe: 'Well, first of all she should be a woman.'

* * *

Gurruld: '— as the clergyman said, "I now pronounce you man and wife and I leave it to yourselves to discover which is which."'

* * *

Basil: '— and then there was the girl with the st-st-st-stammer who was t-t-trying to say that she w-w-wasn't that sort of gug-gug-girl, but she was before she could get it out.'

* * *

Trevor: 'And of course there was the girl who thought a brothel was a new kind of soup.'

* * *

Robert: 'We took Ned the Gom to the show in the Cork Opera House the other night, and he was thrown out for speaking to his father.'

Us: 'That was a bit hard.'
Robert: 'Well, of course we were in the upper circle, and his
           da was in the stalls.

                    *   *   *

Burko cracked a joke the other night—the end of the world
must be coming, or at least the end of the book—

Burko: 'The doctor called to see a man that I know, and
           told the man's wife that he had rigor mortis.
           "Is that serious," said the wife.
           "Well," said the doctor, "he'll feel a little stiff in the
           morning".'

                    *   *   *

           There was a spider on the wall
           He had no hair on his body at all
           No brush, no comb to comb his hair —
           He *had* no hair — what the hell did he care?

                    *   *   *

Harry: Have ye no homes to go to?

CLOSING TIME